S0-BOF-906

DATE DUE

~~APR 2 3~~			
~~AP 23~~ '04			
Madison 4-4-06 McInnis			
'APR 5'			
~~AG 2 0~~			

DEMCO NO. 38 - 2980

BATTLES
THAT CHANGED THE WORLD

FIRST BATTLE OF THE MARNE

GETTYSBURG

HASTINGS

MARATHON

MIDWAY

NORMANDY

SARATOGA

TENOCHTITLAN

TET OFFENSIVE

WATERLOO

The
Norman
Conquest:
1066

HASTINGS

SAMUEL WILLARD CROMPTON

CHELSEA HOUSE PUBLISHERS
PHILADELPHIA

FRONTIS: This map shows the major scenes of action in the year 1066. The Norman invasion route is shown at center-right. The Norse invasion is not shown, but the city of York, at top-center is near the Battle of Stamford Bridge.

942.02
Cr
3/03

CHELSEA HOUSE PUBLISHERS

EDITOR IN CHIEF Sally Cheney
DIRECTOR OF PRODUCTION Kim Shinners
CREATIVE MANAGER Takeshi Takahashi
MANUFACTURING MANAGER Diann Grasse

STAFF FOR HASTINGS

EDITOR Lee Marcott
ASSOCIATE EDITOR Bill Conn
PICTURE RESEARCHER Sarah Bloom
PRODUCTION ASSISTANT Jaimie Winkler
COVER AND SERIES DESIGNER Keith Trego
LAYOUT 21st Century Publishing and Communications, Inc.

http://www.chelseahouse.com

First Printing

1 3 5 7 9 8 6 4 2

Library of Congress Cataloging-in-Publication Data

Crompton, Samuel Willard.
   Hastings / Samuel Willard Crompton.
      p. cm. — (Battles that changed the world)
Summary: Provides a historical account of the 1066 Battle of Hastings, a pivotal event in England's history, as well as the people and events leading up to it and its ramifications. Includes bibliographical references and index.
   ISBN 0-7910-6680-0 HC ISBN 0-7910-7164-2 PB
  1. Hastings, Battle of, 1066—Juvenile literature. [1. Hastings, Battle of, 1066. 2. Great Britain—History—William I, 1066-1087.] I. Title. II. Series.
DA196 .C76 2002
942.02'1—dc21

                                                                    2002003714

CONTENTS

Viking raids against Europe began around A.D. 800 and reached their climax early in the 11th century. The Vikings were renowned for the speed of their attacks, and the swiftness with which they extricated themselves from difficult situations.

Angles, Saxons, and Vikings:
The Island Kingdom between A.D. 400 and 1000

Alfred, son of Aethelwulf, passed away six nights before All Saints' Day. He was king over all the English except for that part which was under Danish rule; and he held that kingdom for one and a half years less than thirty.

–The *Anglo-Saxon Chronicle* (A.D. 900)

England is a land of sheep and meadows, the home of the legendary King Arthur and the historical King Alfred, the birthplace of the Anglo-Saxon common law and the jury system, and the starting point for a language spoken around the world in the 21st century.

How did England become the England that we know today? Who were its peoples, leaders, and what were the events that bound this island nation together and made it so important in the history of Western civilization? Not all, but some of the answers can be found by studying the years between A.D. 1000 and A.D. 1086, with a special emphasis on the pivotal year A.D. 1066.

The people living in England around the year 1000 were the recipients of a culture that had developed over the past 1,000 years, and which showed a mixture of Briton, Roman, Anglo-Saxon, and Danish elements.

The Britons, about whom we know rather little, were conquered by the Romans during the reign of Emperor Claudius; the southern half of what is now England became a Roman province. Scotland and Ireland, however, were never conquered by the Romans. Julius Caesar and other Romans condemned the Britons for practicing human sacrifices and ritualistic body painting.

The Romans ruled England until about 410, when Rome withdrew her legions. It was an essential move at the time, since the Roman Empire was being attacked in other parts of the world. However, many Britons had long since become accustomed to Roman government and felt betrayed by the Roman departure. The island was left unprotected, and was soon invaded by a number of Germanic tribes, including the Angles, Saxons, and Jutes.

The Angles (who lent their name to the land) and Saxons became the dominant tribes in the takeover of England. Although his existence cannot be verified by history, many people believe that a British chief named Arthur fought the Angles and Saxons for many years, and that he maintained a court called "Camelot," where daring and worthy knights continued the tradition of knighthood and chivalry.

Whether Arthur and his court were real or imaginary, England became a land populated by the Angles, Saxons,

Arthur and Alfred

England has many heroes, but Arthur and Alfred stand at the very top of the list.

Whether he was real, or an imaginary figure, King Arthur stands for much that is good and noble in the English mind. He fought the invaders (Anglo-Saxons). He defended women and the Church, and required his knights to do the same. His knights gathered at the Round Table, which symbolized the perfect equality under which they were expected to live. Arthur was also a tragic figure. He was a cuckolded husband, and the affair between his best knight and his queen led to the breakup of the Round Table. All the same, legend claims that Arthur is sleeping under the English soil and will rise again to defend it when necessary.

Alfred, by contrast, is a known, historical figure. He stands for that quintessentially English type of hero: a man at home with books and swords. Alfred was a devout Christian. He visited Rome in his youth and later wrote Church histories. He was also a man of action. He fought the Danes for many years and restricted the amount of territory they controlled in England. With Alfred, we can start to claim that there truly was an "English" monarchy rather than just a king in Wessex.

Arthur is a distant father figure, one who will come and rescue the nation in the future. Alfred is a comparatively human and warm figure, who appears to have done his work already. Between them, these two men stand for much that the English admire.

and Jutes. Their descendants mixed and mingled with each other and the remaining Britons. By about the eighth century, there was a distinct "English people." They contributed to the spread of Christianity, and the illuminated manuscripts of the English monasteries were famed throughout the Christian world. The most famous of the monasteries was at Lindisfarne, on the northeast coast. One English monk, the Venerable Bede, even contributed the concept of dating years from the birth of Christ.

Anglo-Saxon and Christian England came under attack again toward the end of the eighth century. In 793, Vikings from Scandinavia descended on the monastery at Lindisfarne, which began 300 years of Scandinavian influence on English history. The *Anglo-Saxon Chronicle*, a text composed by monks that serves as one of the most important sources of early English history, stated: "In this year fierce, foreboding omens came over the land of Northumbria, and wretchedly terrified the people . . . The ravaging of heathen men destroyed God's church at Lindisfarne through brutal robbery and slaughter."

"Viking," "Scandinavian," "Norse," and "Northmen," can all be used to describe the peoples who spread terror throughout northern Europe during this period. Sometimes one can be even more specific and refer to Swedes, Danes, and Norwegians. When no other word will do, however, the old standby of "Viking" will be employed. The word "Viking" conjures up images of ships, fire, smoke, violence, and cruelty. However, a closer examination of the Vikings and their history will reveal the motivation for their violent raids

Viking raids began in the middle and later part of the eighth century. Perhaps this was because of a food shortage in Scandinavia—the population had outgrown its food supply. Also, it is possible that the Scandinavians' nautical adventures simply evolved into piracy and terror. In either case, they began to attack the coastlines of England, Scotland, Ireland, Holland, Germany, and France.

Not only did the Norsemen attack unexpectedly, but they also brought a group of warriors called "berserkers," who used both religious fervor and drunken mania to intimidate their opponents. Berserkers lunged into battle carrying great double-handed axes, and calling on the aid of the gods Thor, Odin, Loki, and others. There was something so terrifying about these men that few could withstand them, and many fled instead of facing the Vikings.

This helmet is from a pre-Viking grave at Vendel, Sweden from the 7th century. The helmet and its early date show that the Scandinavian peoples were skillful warriors even before they became Viking marauders.

France and Germany suffered after the death of the Emperor Charlemagne in 814. Charlemagne's grandsons split their lands into three parts in 843, weakening the empire and making it vulnerable to the Scandinavian attacks. By about 900, most of northern Europe appeared helpless before the continuing attacks from the north.

England was saved by the grace and works of King Alfred. Born around 849, Alfred was the youngest son of the

King Alfred the Great of Wessex founded the English Navy. Here the English meet and defeat a group of Danish longboats at Swanage in Dorset. Alfred's successes allowed the Kings of Wessex to gain primacy over the other Anglo-Saxon leaders in England.

king of Wessex. Through a series of accidents and surprises he became king, and he set out to rid the land of the Danes, who had come in force during the last 50 or so years.

The situation was so bad for Alfred and for Wessex that many English lords paid the "danegeld," a specified amount of gold paid as yearly tribute to the Danish pirates. If they thought this would deter future Danish invasions, the nobles were completely mistaken. Coming as they did from the nautical countries of Denmark and Norway, the Scandinavians saw England as a wonderful base from which they could assail other European nations. Therefore, many Danes settled in southern England and became uneasy neighbors of the Anglo-Saxons.

Alfred fought valiantly against the Danes, and he was able to even the playing field for the English. He founded the English navy, in order to fight some of the Danes before they were able to reach his beloved England. By the time he died in 899, Alfred had been able to restrict the Danes to a much smaller section of England than they had previously possessed.

By the time of Alfred's death, the English people considered him and his descendants the guardians of the Anglo-Saxon heritage. During the next 60 years, his successors were able to spread their influence and become truly "kings of England," rather than "kings of Wessex." By about 960, the realm of the English kings extended from Land's End in Cornwall to Dover and Canterbury in the east, and north as far as Berwick-on-Tweed. The king of Scotland and the king of Wales each accepted that the king of England was, to some extent, their overlord. Therefore, something approximating the Kingdom of England had been created.

The measure of security created by King Alfred and his successors was seriously threatened toward the end of the tenth century. The accession to the throne of King Ethelred, often known as "Ethelred the Unready," brought dangerous times to the island kingdom. "Unready" meant "unadvised" or "badly advised," and Ethelred truly lived up to this name.

King Ethelred the Unready reigned from 978-1016. As the portrait shows, Ethelred was not cowardly or shrinking. The expression "Unready" probably meant "Uncounseled" or "Badly Advised."

Danes and Normans:
England and Her Neighbors between 1000 and 1064

That same spring, the lady Ymma Aelfgyfu, Richard's daughter, came to this land.

—The *Anglo-Saxon Chronicle* (1002)

King Ethelred, often called "the Unready," was not a warrior king in the tradition of his ancestors. During his long reign (978-1014), England was threatened by numerous invasions, most of them originating in Denmark. In the year 1000, the *Anglo-Saxon Chronicle* declared: "The king went into Cumberland and ravaged very nearly all of it. His ships went out around Chester and should have come to meet him, but they could not; then they ravaged the Isle of Man. The enemy fleet had turned that summer to Richard's kingdom in Normandy."

In the case above, in the *Anglo-Saxon Chronicle* entry for the year 1000, the King is Ethelred the Unready. The foes he seeks out are Danish pirates who are committing depredations on the English coastline. The reference to "Richard's kingdom" connotes the dukedom of Normandy, which was part of the kingdom of France.

As the entry shows, England was no stranger to hostile sea born attacks. She had suffered numerous times from Viking invasions.

The Danes continued their attacks, and in 1002 the *Anglo-Saxon Chronicle* declares:

> The king and counselors advised that tribute be yielded to the seamen and peace made with them, on the condition that they should leave off their evil doing . . . They accepted that, and were at that time given twenty-four thousand pounds. During these events, ealdorman Leofsige killed Aefic, the king's high-reeve, and the king banished him from the land. That same spring, the lady Ymma Aelfgyfu, Richard's daughter, came to this land.

The 24,000 pounds became known as the "danegeld," the tribute money paid by England to the Danish pirates. Equally important was the appearance of Ymma (Emma), who married King Ethelred and became England's queen. She was daughter of Duke Richard of Normandy, also known as Richard the Fearless, and her marriage to Ethelred in 1002 would provide the pretext for a later Norman presence, and even later a Norman invasion of England.

Normandy (meaning "land-of-the-northmen") was one of the French duchies. It had been created in the year 911 when King Charles III of France (often called Charles the Simple) had made a deal with a Norwegian Viking named

Rollo. The Norwegians had arrived in France one or two years earlier, and, unlike many Vikings, had chosen to stay. Rollo had made camp near the mouth of the Seine River, and King Charles decided to befriend this Viking, rather than try to expel him. In 911, Rollo and King Charles agreed to the treaty of Sur-Le-Epte, which made Rollo a vassal of the king of France and duke of Normandy.

Rollo was succeeded by his son William Longsword, who was followed by Duke Richard the Fearless, who was succeeded by his son, Duke Richard II. During the rule of Richard II, Emma, who was Richard's sister, was married to King Ethelred of England. It was the first time in over a century that the English monarchy looked outside of the kingdom for a bride, and the marriage had long-lasting consequences.

Emma and King Ethelred appear to have made a poor match. Although they had two children—Edgar and Edward—there was little love between the royal couple, and their animosity helped to deprive England of strong leadership when the country sorely needed it.

England was soon threatened by the Danes once more, and this time the Danes had it in their mind to take the whole country. The *Anglo-Saxon Chronicle* describes the savagery with which the Danes attacked:

> Cnut came with his force, and ealdorman Eadric with him, across the Tames into Mercia at Cricklade. They went into Warwickshire during the season of Christmas, and ravaged, burnt, and killed all they came across . . . Then it befell that King Aethelred passed away before the ships arrived; he ended his days on St. George's Day, after much trouble and wretchedness in his life

The name of the Danish leader was Cnut, which his English foes lengthened to Canute. Ruler of Denmark, he was a fierce and cunning warrior who planned his invasions well in advance and generally out-scouted, as well as out-fought, his enemies.

King Ethelred was dead by the time Canute landed in England in 1015. Canute was left to face Edmund Ironsides, a skillful and charismatic leader who would lead the Anglo-Saxons against Canute and the Danes. After Edmund died in battle in 1016, both his son and Ethelred's sons went into exile. There was no one left for Canute to fight.

Canute became king of England. To all observers, it was apparent that the line of Cedric, passed through King Alfred and his descendants, was finished as the ruling house of England. The island kingdom seemed fated to become part of a new Scandinavian-Anglo empire, ruled by Canute.

Canute knew the wisdom of maintaining some English traditions. One year after his takeover, Canute married Queen Emma, the widow of King Ethelred. She had given Ethelred two sons, both of whom were now in exile. She appeared happier with Canute than she had been with Ethelred, and the couple had two sons, Harthacanute and Harold. Thus, Emma, a Norman noblewoman, had provided England with four potential heirs, two of whom were from the ancient line of King Alfred, and two of whom were from the new line of Canute.

Given all the confusion and conflict, it would seem natural that King Canute would have a difficult and fractured reign. However, just the opposite occurred. Canute turned out to be the most effective and the most balanced ruler England had had in two generations. As the years passed, Canute sent most of his Danish army home, and ruled with only the protection of his housecarls. These formidable ax-wielding soldiers were the core of Canute's strength, and later they became central to the Anglo-Saxon army.

Cnut (or Canute) was the greatest Danish leader of the 11th century. He conquered southern England and married Ymma Aelfgyfu, the widow of King Ethelred. The new couple were a successful love match. Here they place a cross on the altar of the New Minster at Winchester.

Canute showed himself to be skillful in diplomacy and adroit in governing. One of the most interesting tales told of Canute is that one day he was on the shore, sitting on a makeshift throne near the water. Canute pointed out the rising tide to his advisers standing with him. Some of them fatuously commented that Canute was so wise and powerful that even the sea must obey his commands. Mocking them, Canute ordered the rising tide to reverse itself and become an ebbing tide. When the water continued to advance and lapped around the king's feet, Canute turned to his advisers and pointed out the limits that even the strongest and best king must accept.

Canute died in 1035. Though precedence should have gone to his son Harthacanute by Queen Emma, a dispute ensued between Harthacanute and his brother Harold. For a time the kingdom was ruled jointly. Neither of these rulers fared very well, and they died young. In 1042 the throne was offered to Prince Edward, son of Emma and King Ethelred, who had spent many years in exile in Normandy.

Among Canute's relatives in Denmark, the story spread that the throne of Canute should go to one of the family. King Magnus of Denmark did not take advantage of this claim, but a later king, Harald, would do so.

Edward took the throne, and governed with a modicum of good sense and balance. His subjects noted his pious behavior and soon called him "Edward the Confessor." Edward took care not to offend his Danish subjects, and he may have taken for granted the loyalty of his Anglo-Saxons. But Edward showed his strongest preference for Norman counselors and Norman architects. Since he spent so many years in Normandy and his mother was a Norman, King Edward continued to show this predilection throughout his reign.

Yet Edward certainly could not afford to alienate the high men of the land: the earls of England. One of the

Edward the Confessor was crowned at Winchester Cathedral by Eadsipe, the Archbishop of Canterbury. Edward was of the ancient line of Wessex, but he had spent many years as a political exile in Normandy. Throughout his reign, Edward favored Normans, both as churchmen and as political councillors.

Emma and Edith

Two of the most important women in 11th century England were Emma of Normandy and Edith, daughter of Godwin. Each of them had a profound influence on King Edward the Confessor, and each of them contributed to the political vision of the times.

Daughter of Duke Richard the Fearless, Emma went to England in 1002 to marry King Ethelred. Theirs was not a happy marriage, and she may have been pleased when Ethelred died, and the Danish leader Canute became the new king of England. She married Canute in 1017. This was a happy union, marred only by the resentment of Ethelred's two sons. Emma possessed considerable influence during Canute's reign, but that ended in 1042 when her son, Edward the Confessor, became king. One of his first acts was to dispossess his mother of nearly all her property. Some historians believe her neglect of Edward made him ambivalent toward women for the rest of his life. Emma died in Winchester in 1052. She was buried next to her second husband, Canute.

In 1045 King Edward the Confessor married Edith, one of the daughters of Earl Godwin. The couple appeared to have lacked passion for each other, and the king was heard to refer to the queen as his "sister." But any thought of disregard between the two passed after King Edward's death in 1066. Queen Edith wrote a stirring and compelling history of her husband's life and reign, leaving no doubt she favored him above all other men.

most powerful of them was a man named Godwin, who became Earl of Wessex, second only to the king in power and importance.

Very little is known about Godwin. His foes often claimed he was the son of a Danish sheep herder, and that may have been true. But through the force of his personality, Godwin had thrived during the reign of Canute, then of Harthacanute, and now he became chief counselor to King Edward.

Godwin's daughter, Edith, married the king in 1045. King Edward seemed to have liked his bride well enough, but had an aversion to marital relations. The couple never had any children. That was harmless enough in the early years of his reign, but as time passed, anxiety grew over who would eventually succeed the king.

King Edward's father-in-law, Godwin, passed away in 1053, but the family of Godwin continued to influence the king and kingdom. Many people believed that Harold, oldest of the sons of Godwin, would attempt to take the throne upon King Edward's death. Others feared that the King's death might bring on a civil war between the House of Godwin and the House of Leofric, which controlled the other earldoms. There were even contenders from outside the land. Duke William of Normandy claimed he was the true successor to King Edward; the two men were first cousins once removed. And far to the east in frozen Norway, King Harald Hardrada also claimed the throne should be his.

Lord, Vassal, and Oath:
The Bayeux Tapestry and the Oath of Earl Harold to Duke William

The Bayeux Tapestry is the single most important source for understanding the year 1066. Here, King Edward the Confessor sends Earl Harold Godwinsson on a diplomatic mission to Normandy.

Ubi Harold sacramentum fecit VVillelmo Duci
Where Harold made an oath to Duke William

–The Bayeux Tapestry

The Bayeux Tapestry is 230 feet long and from 10 1/4 to 19 3/4 inches wide. Today it is displayed in the Central Museum of Bayeux. The tapestry winds completely around the room, giving the observer a complete view of the Norman interpretation of the Conquest of 1066.

It is not known who conceived the idea of the Bayeux Tapestry, much less who sewed the cloth, but it seems to have been made within 20 years of the Norman Conquest and commissioned by Bishop Odo, a half-brother of Duke William. Recent scholarship suggests it was made by English hands, and then brought to Bayeux, where it remained undisturbed for centuries. The first official notice was made of it in 1472, but it was not studied or written about until the 18th century.

The tapestry illustrates 626 human figures, 190 horses or mules, 35 hounds or dogs, 506 other animals, 37 ships, 33 buildings, and 37 trees or groups of trees. Inscriptions run underneath and there is a 3- to 4-inch border both at the top and bottom.

The story depicted on the tapestry begins with King Edward the Confessor instructing Earl Harold (notice the difference between "Harold" of England and "Harald" of Norway). It is unclear what the instructions are, but the next three pictures give some clues. A party of mounted men led by Earl Harold set off for the coast. Harold has a hawk on his wrist and hounds in front of his horse, indicating that he is on an expedition meant for pleasure.

The story then proceeds to Bosham near Chichester in Sussex. This was Earl Harold's manor home, and the scene shows Harold and a friend praying at Bosham Church. The scene is enigmatic. Does it mean to suggest that Harold felt himself in some danger or that he was a pious person of the times?

Next the tapestry shows us a group of retainers feasting at Harold's manor house. Cups, which are rather like bowls, and horns of wine are passed back and forth, and most of the feasters seem thoroughly engrossed. But one person on the far right points to the coast, indicating that it is time to embark. Again, the tapestry is less than clear. Was Harold proceeding on a journey that King Edward commanded? Or was this a journey for pleasure?

The Bayeux Tapestry

France was in grave danger in 1792. The French Revolution, which had begun in 1789, was judged to be a threat to the other European monarchies. Austria and Prussia had declared war on Revolutionary France, and the Revolutionary leaders sent out a call to every village, town, and city in the nation.

In the town of Bayeux, Normandy, a group of volunteers came to answer the call. As they were about to leave for a military camp, someone declared that they had insufficient packing cloth to cover the supply wagons. Someone else mentioned the venerable tapestry within the town cathedral. Perhaps it might be pulled out and used to cover the wagons.

The Bayeux Tapestry, which had been in existence for about 700 years, was pulled out of the church and put across a group of wagons. The convoy was about to depart when Monsieur Leonard-Leforestier, a respected lawyer, appeared. He addressed the crowd of volunteers and persuaded them that this historic tapestry should not be used as a tarpaulin. The crowd relented, and the tapestry was removed from the wagon. Leforestier took it to his office for safekeeping, and when the military emergency had ended, he gave it back to the care of the town administrators.

Thus was saved one of the great relics of French and English history. Because of the tapestry, today we have a much better knowledge of the remarkable events that transpired in England and Normandy, between 1064 and 1066.

We cannot be sure.

Carrying hawks and hounds, Harold and his companions wade out to their ship, which resembles the Viking long ship of that era. The English group gets under way by using poles and oars, indicating the shoal water and sluggish currents of that area.

The square sail is spread, and the party makes full

The Bayeux Tapestry shows Earl Harold's party landing on the shore of Normandy. Harold stands in the bow of the foremost ship. The scene does not show that Harold was immediately arrested and imprisoned by the local nobleman, Count Guy of Ponthieu.

sail. For the first time in their journey, the English have a definite or united air about them; prior to this they looked uncertain and divided.

The ship nears the French coast, and a sailor prepares to drop the anchor. The ship is then shown dismasted and securely anchored on shore.

So far, there is no large surprise. This could have been one of any number of times that Earl Harold took a sail up or down the English Channel. But, Count Guy of Ponthieu appears and seizes Harold and his men. The count is a vassal of the duke of Normandy, and one would not expect him to boldly sequester one of the leading men of England, but the tapestry shows the scene in full light.

This scene prompts one of the most important questions thus far in the Bayeux Tapestry's story: why did Count Guy seize Earl Harold? Yes, there was a law concerning shipwrecks on shore, but that does not seem to apply to Harold; his ship had safely landed. Where, then, did Count Guy obtain the authority to seize Harold?

We are reduced to conjecture. It may be that Duke William empowered the count to seize the earl. Then again, it may have simply been a mistake. But the next scene depicts Harold imprisoned by Count Guy.

The story takes us next to Duke William's court at Rouen. Upon learning of Harold's seizure, William sets out and meets the Count, with his prisoner, at the border between their lands. Count Guy delivers Earl Harold to Duke William, and, had events been normal, that might have been the end of the matter.

However, this is not the case. Harold is brought to Rouen. He is no longer in prison, but he appears unable to leave. For better or worse, he has become part of Duke William's court and retinue.

The tapestry has a scene where Duke William sits on a throne, looking stern and grave, while Earl Harold makes an impassioned speech. It is unclear whether Harold is asking for his freedom, or whether he is asking permission for something else. But the seating arrangement and the position of the characters show that William was in the superior position and that Harold was the supplicant.

The tapestry moves next to a military campaign. Duke William leads Norman troops south to attack the Count of Brittany. The tapestry shows us that Earl Harold goes with Duke William; a scene depicts the Norman army crossing the river near Mont Saint-Michel. (This is the first representation of the famous monastery anywhere in medieval art.)

As they cross the river, two of Duke William's men are trapped in quicksand and are likely to die. The tapestry shows Earl Harold jump in after the men and save them. If this happened, it clearly shows Harold to have been a man of boldness and impetuosity: two characteristics which William may have noted for later reference.

The military campaign concludes successfully, and the tapestry takes us back to Normandy, where Duke William bestows arms upon Earl Harold. This scene, which shows the duke on the left and the earl to right, is one of the most important. If William did this, it made Harold his liege man and vassal. Medieval society took oaths of fealty very seriously, and Duke William may have been convinced that from that day Harold would be his vassal.

However, what remains unknown is why an earl from England would become the vassal of a Norman duke.

The climactic scene of Harold's time in Normandy comes in plate 29 of the Bayeux Tapestry. As before, Duke William is enthroned, but in an awkward position. His feet come together on a narrow base, making William look like a double triangle. Harold is in an equally awkward position, as he stands in the middle of the drawing with his right hand stretched toward one altar and his left hand extended to another. Between these two altars stands Harold, pulled in two directions at once. The caption reads: *"Ubi Harold sacramentum fecit VVillelmo Duci"* ("Where Harold made an oath to Duke William").

The tapestry does not tell us what the oath was for

The Lord-Vassal Relationship

The early Middle Ages, roughly from A.D. 600 to 1000, were dangerous times. Vikings, Magyar horsemen, and Muslim pirates all threatened Europe: the Vikings from the north, the Magyars from the east, and the Muslims from the south and southeast.

Because of these attacks, Europe developed the lord-vassal relationship which was the cornerstone of the feudal system.

A lord and vassal swore oaths in a ceremony together. The lord swore to protect his vassal, his vassal's land, his crops, and his family. The vassal swore to be the liege man of the lord: to serve in the lord's army if necessary, and to yield to him a portion of his crop, often a one-third share. The ceremony was binding on both parties, and medieval Europeans were scandalized when people broke their oaths.

The system worked well for some time. Vassals were able to grow more food because they were protected by the lords. The lord's one-third share of the food consequently grew. Invaders were more effectively pushed away, and European security began to grow; so too did its population.

However, the system was not without its flaws. Occasionally a vassal would swear allegiance to two different lords. If these lords battled each other, the vassal would be forced to break his sacred oath with one of the lords, and support the other.

In the special case of Harold and William, there was an additional complication. As an Englishman, Earl Harold already owed allegiance to King Edward and the English government. Therefore, Harold could and did disregard the oath he had made to Duke William when the Anglo-Saxon *witan* (council of nobles) named Harold king in January 1066.

because the people who made the tapestry did so after 1066, when nearly everyone would have known the Norman interpretation of events. According to written sources, Earl Harold swore he would support Duke William's right to the English throne upon the death of King Edward the Confessor.

bAROLD:SACRAMENTVM:FECIT:⸱ hIC
VVILLELMO DVCI:⸱

This scene from the Bayeux Tapestry shows the climactic moment in which Earl Harold, with one hand on each of the two sacred relics, swears an oath of fealty to Duke William of Normandy. The Normans rested their case for William's accession to the throne of England on this particular event.

The matter was settled as far as the Normans were concerned.

Harold likely had no choice but to consent to the presentation of arms and the oath of allegiance that made him Duke William's vassal. The code of chivalry and rules of hospitality would have forced him to accept the vassalage.

Harold returned to England. Nearly one year passed without much trouble, but then he was summoned to deal with troubles in Northumbria. A revolt had broken out against his brother Tostig.

The King is Dead; Long Live the King:
King Edward, Earl Harold, and Earl Tostig

King Edward the Confessor died on January 5, 1066. Because he never had a son, the realm was in danger of conflict and tumult over who should succeed him as King of England.

Who, when he was gone, should wear the royal crown of England, the imperial diadem of Britain? Eadward, at that last moment, was not wanting to his last duty. He stretched forth his hand toward the Earl of West-Saxons and spake the words, "To thee, Harold my brother, I commit my kingdom."

—History of the Norman Conquest of England

Tostig, the third-youngest son of Godwin, made a name for himself early in life. Like his older brother Harold, Tostig was known as an excellent warrior. The two brothers had worked together to defeat the Welsh just a few years earlier.

But Tostig was quite unlike Harold in that he was unable to control his temper. Tostig had become Earl of Northumbria in 1055, but he had succeeded in alienating many of his subjects.

Northumbria lay between the English midlands and the border with Scotland. Some people still called it "Danelaw," referring to the many Danes who had settled there in the ninth and tenth centuries. The people of Northumbria had to be hardy and tough, as they were often beset by Viking and Scottish raids.

Tostig was a hard and unfeeling earl. A revolt against him began in January 1065, and accelerated throughout the spring and summer. Tostig, who was on excellent terms with King Edward, convinced the king that the rebels should be dealt with firmly. King Edward then summoned the man whom he could most trust to delve into the situation: Earl Harold of Wessex.

Although he was his brother, Earl Harold soon concluded that Tostig had been a difficult ruler in Northumbria. Tostig had forced the people to give up the aspects of Danish law that had been part of their cultural heritage; he had insisted on the primacy of Anglo-Saxon law. In a kingdom as diverse and eclectic as England, this type of move toward centralization may have been seen as an asset by some, but it also provoked considerable resistance.

No record exists of the meeting between King Edward, Earl Harold, and Earl Tostig. But the result was that King Edward agreed to the rebels' terms. Tostig was stripped of his status as earl; the rebels were pardoned, and accepted the rule of Morcar, their new leader.

Tostig returned to London, packed his bags, and departed for Flanders with his wife and family. There, his wife's half-brother, Count Baldwin, offered them safe shelter. But Tostig burned for revenge on his brother,

The Family of Godwin

Considering how important he was in mid-century English history, we know rather little about Earl Godwin. He was a shadowy figure during the reign of King Canute, and he emerged as a powerful man during the reign of King Edward the Confessor. Godwin and his large family were exiled by King Edward in 1051, but they returned in 1052. Godwin died a year later, leaving two daughters and seven sons.

- Edith, oldest of the daughters, married King Edward the Confessor.
- Sweyn, oldest of the sons, disgraced himself, and went into exile.
- Harold succeed his father as earl of Wessex.
- Tostig became earl of Northumbria.
- Gyrth became earl of East Anglia.
- Leofwin became earl of the Southeast Midlands.
- Wulfnoth and Gunnhild were the youngest, and did not succeed to any major positions.

When we consider that people thought Godwin the father was a parvenu (newcomer), it is astonishing to what degree he succeeded in inserting his family into top positions in the land. His success and that of his children provoked envy and suspicion among other leaders in England.

and it was not long before circumstances afforded him an opportunity to strike.

King Edward sickened and worsened as the year 1065 came to its end. On December 28, the new church at Westminster was consecrated. The building of the church had been one of the projects dearest to King Edward's heart, but he was too ill to attend the ceremony. His condition continued to worsen, and the Anglo-Saxon witan was called to be present in the event of the king's death.

On the morning of January 4, 1066, King Edward was near death. In his last hours he was accompanied by Earl Harold and Stigand, the archbishop of Canterbury. The dying king uttered some words of prophecy, most of which sounded very dark. The archbishop shook his head in dismissal of the words, but then the talk passed to the heart of the matter:

> At last Harold and Stigand—nor have we any right to exclude Robert from their counsels—found means of calling Eadward's mind to the great subject which then filled the whole heart of England. When all was over, when his body was laid in the new minster, when his soul had gone to its reward, who should fill the place which he had so long filled on earth? Who, when he was gone, should wear the royal crown of England, the Imperial diadem of Britain? Eadward, at that last moment, was not wanting to his last duty. He stretched forth his hand towards the Earl of the West-Saxons, and spake the words, 'To thee, Harold my brother, I commit my Kingdom'

Edward and Harold were not brothers but brothers-in-law. The king had spoken. He died an hour or two later, and the word was quickly passed to the members of the witan that King Edward had chosen Earl Harold to be his successor.

Had England been a continental kingdom, like France, Hungary, or Navarre, Edward's words would have been sufficient. But, just as England did not eagerly follow the pope's lead in religious matters, so it did not follow the continental view of absolute succession from father to son, or from dying monarch to the one named. England's Anglo-Saxon traditions, embodied in the presence of the witan, derived more from the Germanic idea of tribal

King Edward was burled at Westminster Abbey on the morning of January 6, 1066. The abbey—which Edward had funded—had just been dedicated ten days earlier.

kingship. The council of the nobles would vote on whether to accept the dying king's chosen successor.

It is not known whether the debate was long and impassioned or whether there was a close vote. All that is known is that by the end of that day, the witan had confirmed Edward the Confessor's choice; Earl Harold of Wessex was to be the new king of England.

Some historians point out that the witan had been hastily assembled; had its full quota of members been present, especially those from Northumbria, Harold might have encountered more resistance. Be that as it may, the choice was made. King Edward was buried on the morning of January 6, 1065 the Feast of the Epiphany, and Earl Harold was anointed and crowned king of England that

Harold Godwinsson was crowned King of England in the afternoon of January 6, 1066. He was not related to King Edward, but Harold had been the king's right-hand man for the past decade. Harold had also been chosen by the Anglo-Saxon *witan*.

afternoon. So far as the witan was concerned, the matter was closed.

There were three other men for whom the matter was not settled: Duke William of Normandy, Earl Tostig in exile, and King Harald Hardrada of Norway.

Duke William claimed the English throne on two counts. First, he was a first cousin, once removed, of the deceased Edward the Confessor. Second, Duke William claimed that Earl Harold had made an oath of allegiance to him, two years past. If this were true, then Harold should relinquish the throne to William.

If Harold had sworn such an oath, then there is little doubt that Duke William was the person who possessed the best *claim* to the throne of England.

Earl Tostig had no legal or constitutional right to the English throne. Tostig wanted revenge on his brother Harold. Because of his relationship to the count of Flanders, through his marriage, Tostig had the potential to bring large forces to bear against Harold. Of the different men who laid claim to the English throne, Tostig was the most *driven,* sometimes to the point of foolhardiness.

The third man who claimed the throne was by far the most fearsome. Harald Hardrada had been king of Norway for 18 years. Prior to that he had been a Viking warrior, selling his services to Russian dukes, and then to the Empress Irene in Constantinople. As leader of the Varangian Guard (a special bodyguard composed entirely of Viking or Scandinavian warriors), Harald had fought battles in Turkey, on the Mediterranean, and in Sicily and Italy as well. By the time he returned to become king of Norway, Harald was the most feared warrior in western and northern Europe. Nothing he had done since then had diminished his reputation.

If Harald were to turn to England, he could bring the fury of the Northmen down upon the Anglo-Saxon Kingdom. If there was one person who had the potential to take England by *force*, it was Harald.

Which of these four men would prevail? Harold? William? Tostig? Or Harald?

The Bayeux Tapestry shows the appearance of a fiery comet that appeared over England in April 1066. As the gestures made by the men at left indicate, the comet was seen as a bad omen for Harold and his reign.

The Comet's Eye

Then it happened that all through England such a sign in the heavens was seen as no man had seen before. Some men said that it was the star, 'Comet,' that some men call the long-haired star.

—The *Anglo-Saxon Chronicle* (1066)

D uke William was hunting outside the town of Rouen when he heard the news of King Edward's death and the coronation of Harold. His attendants report that he stopped his day's hunt, spoke to no one, and went to his nearby castle where he brooded for hours. When a nobleman was bold enough to speak to him hours later, the Duke had decided to mount a campaign against Harold.

As is sometimes the case with great and ambitious men, it is difficult to know how much of their appearance is contrived and how much is heartfelt. Duke William may well have been upset that the oath of fealty Harold once swore to him had been violated, but a man as ambitious as the duke must have suspected that Harold would not turn down a kingdom when it was offered. We do not know how much of William's anger was genuine, or to what extent it was designed to win over the support of the Norman nobles.

As furious as he may have been, William knew he could not simply command his Norman knights to cross the Channel. They were under no obligation to serve elsewhere. If he wanted them to follow him to England, he would have to win them to his cause.

One way to do so was to appeal to their Christian faith. Here, William held a trump card: his friendship with Lanfranc, Bishop of Bec, which gave him unusually good access to the pope in Rome. Pope Alexander II had studied at the monastery in Bec, 20 years earlier, and he was great friends with Lanfranc, leader of the monks in Normandy. Lanfranc did not take Duke William's case himself, but he sent monks and ambassadors to Rome to defend Duke William's right to England.

Alexander II was the first pope to have been elected by the college of cardinals, created in 1059. Prior to that, popes had been made and unmade by the Holy Roman Emperor, and by a succession created by the popes themselves. The major reforms in the Church that created the college of cardinals had been thoroughly accepted by the Norman clergy, but not by the English monks and priests. Therefore, Pope Alexander II had a very good

Alexander II was the first man to be elected Pope by the College of
Cardinals, which had been created a few years earlier. Alexander
knew little about the affairs of England, but he was inclined to back
the Normans because he had studied at the monastery of Bec in
Normandy many years earlier.

reason to support Duke William, especially since William promised to "clean up" the English Church, to cleanse it of the abuses that some claimed existed.

Making matters even more appealing to Pope Alexander II, Duke William made vague promises to hold all England as a fief of the pope after the land was conquered. If all this came to fulfillment, there would be a new reformed English Church, and all the lands would belong to Pope Alexander II in theory. It is not surprising that Alexander II endorsed William's plan for an invasion of England!

The pope sent a banner, indicating his approval of William's planned invasion. William used the papal flag to good effect at the conferences he held with Norman nobles; it persuaded them to join the invasion. By March of 1066, William had decided to invade and conquer England. He put many of his subjects to work, building large boats to carry his army across the Channel.

Then came the comet.

It was Halley's Comet, which comes every 70 or 75 years. It appeared in the third week of April, and for the following 10 days shone more brightly than any celestial event in memory. The comet also appears in the Bayeux Tapestry. Men point to it and gesture, indicating that the English saw it as an evil omen.

Just days after the comet appeared, trouble appeared on the coast of southern and eastern England. The deposed Earl Tostig had come back to claim vengeance against his brother King Harold.

Tostig caused damage on the English shore. After an especially vicious raid near the mouth of the Thames River, Tostig was attacked and driven off with great losses. He and his remaining men escaped in their ships and went north, where Tostig became a temporary guest of King Malcolm Canmore of Scotland.

Halley's Comet

Chinese chroniclers had noticed the comet as early as 2,200 B.C. The *Anglo-Saxon Chronicle*, too, had observed the comet's appearance in A.D. 995. But the previous appearances did nothing to diminish the fears and anxieties which many people experienced on seeing the comet in April 1066.

Chinese annals also mentioned the appearance of the comet in 1066, but saved their most profound praise for the comet of 1378, saying that "it was equal to the full moon in its size, and its train, at first small, increased to a wonderful length."

The comet returned in 1145, 1223, 1301, 1378, 1456, 1531, 1607, 1682, 1759, 1835, 1910, and 1986. Just as they had in 1066, the observers of the comet in 1759 considered it an omen or foreshadowing of important events to come. In fact, 1759 came to be known as the "Miracle Year" by the English because of the victories they won over the French at Quebec, in India, in Europe, and on the high seas.

The comet's appearance in 1682 led the English astronomer Edmund Halley to investigate records and make an examination of the skies. His observations led to the phenomenon named "Halley's Comet," and the name has stuck ever since.

One prominent American who showed an interest in the comet was the humorist Mark Twain. Born in Missouri in 1835, he believed he "came into the world with Halley's Comet," and that he would go out with it as well. Twain died in 1910, the year that the comet returned.

As much as 21st century Americans understand about science and nature, they too thrill to the sight of a comet streaking across the sky. Sometimes they admire its passing; at other times they act on strange and unusual impulses, attributing those impulses to the pull from the heavens.

Scotland was just emerging from one of the most deadly and divisive periods of its history, and King Malcolm was a new type of Scottish king, one who wanted to keep the peace. However, he was not above creating unhappiness for his southern neighbors. Malcolm entertained Tostig and encouraged him in his hopes to return south and overthrow his brother.

Tostig had made friendly overtures to King Malcolm while he had been earl of Northumbria, and he now hoped that the Scottish king would assist him in his personal war against Harold.

Tostig found King Malcolm less helpful than he had hoped, so he departed. We might expect he would have gone south to seek refuge with Duke William, but Tostig showed the daring that distinguished him. Rather than go to Normandy, Tostig sailed hundreds of miles east and arrived at the court of King Svein of Denmark.

King Svein offered Tostig an earldom in Denmark if he would remain. Tostig replied that he wanted help from Denmark to overthrow his younger brother. Tostig pointed out that Denmark had a long tradition of involvement in English affairs; King Canute had governed both Denmark and England 40 years earlier. According to historians, King Svein replied:

> I am so much a lesser man than my uncle, King Knut, that I can only just hold Denmark against the Norwegians. Old Knut got Denmark by inheritance and won England by conquest, and for a time it looked as if it might cost him his life. Then he gained Norway without any fighting at all. As far as I am concerned, I intend to be guided more by my own limitations than by my Uncle Knut's achievements.

Disgusted by what he considered cowardice, Tostig went on to another court, that of King Harald Hardrada of Norway. Harald was considered the most fearsome warrior of the age. He was 51, and he had raided and warred from the Mediterranean to the North Sea during more than 30 years abroad.

Even given this long and mighty resume, King Harald was at first dubious about Tostig and his proposal. Tostig wanted Harald to provide a fleet and army, and the two leaders would work as partners to subdue England. It seemed to Harald and his advisers that they would do most of the work, and that Tostig, because of his English blood, might make off with the whole of the reward. But Tostig reminded King Harald that he had spent 15 years warring in an effort to take Denmark and had failed. Now England lay ripe for the taking. Harald weighed this proposal and decided in favor of the expedition. A Norse chronicler named Snorri Sturlson kept an account of these events in a book called *Heimskringla:*

> King Harald then sent word throughout Norway, raising a half-levy of the whole army. This was much talked about, and there was great speculation about the outcome of this venture. Some people reckoned up all King Harald's great achievements, and said that nothing would be too difficult for him; but there were others who said that England would be very hard to conquer—it was very populous, and the warriors who were known as the king's housecarls were so valiant that any one of them was worth two of the best men in King Harald's army. Then Marshal Ulf said:

Gladly I'd draw my sword
Once more for my King Harald;
But little use his marshals
Would be on board his longship,
If one of England's warriors
Could deal with two Norwegians.
When I was young my lady,
Things were different then.

As England—consisting of England, Scotland, and Wales—is an island, ships were an integral part of any invasion that might take place. Whether the invaders were Normans (under Duke William), Flemish (under Tostig), or Norwegians (under Harald Hardrada), the invasion would have to come by sea. Given this, it would seem that the powerful English navy gave King Harold an advantage over his foes.

The English navy had its beginnings under King Alfred the Great, more than 150 years earlier. Alfred had seen the importance of fighting Viking raiders before they landed on English soil; he had built up a fleet which was significant through the reign of Edward the Confessor. Even conservative estimates reckon that King Harold had 100 ships of all sizes in his fleet. While that might not be enough to stop a true Viking invasion, such as the one planned in Norway, it was more than sufficient to patrol the southern English coast and keep a sharp lookout for any movement from Normandy.

Just across the Channel, Duke William had his hands full trying to build a fleet. His Norman subjects, accustomed though they were to fighting on land, were now trying to build ships and regain some of the skill of their Viking ancestors. The Bayeux Tapestry depicts men cutting down trees, planing the wood, and building

The Normans were descendants of Vikings, but they had been a land-based people for the 100 years before 1066. They had to relearn the skills needed to build the boats for the invasion of England.

ships. "Boats" might be a better word, since almost none of them were meant to accommodate more than about a dozen men and perhaps two horses.

While the Normans built boats, King Harold mustered the different levels of military men in his kingdom. First and foremost were the housecarls. These were mercenary troops, who had first come to England with the Danish King Canute in 1016. The housecarls were formidable men who rode horses to their battle locations, where they dismounted and fought on foot. Swinging large, double-headed axes, they were the terror of most of their foes and were considered the best personal bodyguard fielded by any king in northern Europe. One can only imagine what a pitched battle between the housecarls and the Varangian Guard of the Byzantine Empire might have been like.

Second, King Harold summoned the English militia, known as the *fyrd*. Under the command of the earls, the fyrd could stay in the field as long as the king needed and as along as food supplies were secure. The militia had seldom been summoned in the past generation, and it was unknown how reliable its members might be.

Third and most comprehensive was the service of every able-bodied adult male in the land. This raising of the land could produce a very large, unwieldy army that could be relied upon only for hours at a time; men had the right to return home each night to tend their farm animals. Unwieldy though this arrangement was, it tended to put the advantage in the hands of the defender in medieval warfare.

Soon after Tostig's raids upon southern England, Harold summoned the fyrd. Militiamen came from all parts of England to garrison forts and watch the coast of Wessex and Sussex. The summer months were better for holding these men to their task, since the spring planting had been done, and fall harvesting had yet to come. So Harold watched and waited. And waited.

Just 60 miles away, Duke William waited as well, for a favorable wind. The boats that had been built were quite seaworthy, but they lacked the ability to sail against the wind. Therefore, William had to wait, and the days turned into weeks.

Neither King Harold nor Duke William were watching the north, where the greatest danger was at that moment.

KONG OLAF.

King Olaf II brought Christianity to Norway. That did not prevent him from being a fearsome warrior and leader, and his younger brother Harald Sigurdsson would be even more of a traditional Viking rover and fighter. Harald went to visit his brother's grave before launching the Norse invasion of England in 1066.

Northmen at York

What will he offer King Harald Sigurdsson for all his effort?

The rider said, "King Harold has already declared how much of England he is prepared to grant him: seven feet of ground, or as much more as he is taller than other men."

–King Harald's Saga

In early summer 1066, King Harald Hardrada sent out a call for the Norwegian Vikings to gather at Solunde Island, north of the present-day city of Bergen at the mouth of the longest and widest fjord in Norway. Harald's reputation as a great warrior and leader was well known in the Viking world at the time, and thousands of Norse warriors came at his summons. By late summer, the Viking host was ready to sail from Solunde.

However, Harald was not yet there. He remained in his capital of Trondheim until the last possible day. Before sailing for Solunde Island, King Harald is said to have entered the shrine to King Olaf, his older half brother, who had died in the Battle of Stiklestad 36 years earlier. Harald had been at the battle with his brother, though he had been only 15 years old. The defeat of the brothers that day had sent Harald on his travels to Russia and the Mediterranean. Now he went to his brother's shrine to receive a blessing.

King Olaf had been the first Christian to rule Norway, and he had converted many members of his court. (Harald was not among them.) Harald entered the shrine and performed rituals that made sense to him, as a pagan, but which may well have offended his Christian brother were he still alive. Harald clipped his nails and offered sacrifices to the dead king. Harald then left, threw the key to the sanctuary into the river, and went quickly to Solunde Island. He brought with him his Russian wife, Elizabeth, and their two daughters. He took his younger son, Olaf, but left his older son, Magnus, behind to serve as king in his absence.

The Viking fleet sailed toward the end of August and landed first in the Shetland Islands, and then the Orkneys, both of which provided more men and supplies. By the time Harald approached the English coast, he had about 240 ships, far and away the largest Viking movement in over 50 years. It was as if Harald would bring back the days when all of Northern Europe trembled at the words "Viking" and "Northmen."

It is unclear whether Tostig was with Harald or

Elizabeth and Thora

Harald Hardrada had two wives: Elizabeth and Thora. The first was the daughter of the Prince of Novgorod (in Russia) and the second was from a prominent Norwegian family.

Harald left Norway in 1030 and spent many years either in Russia or Constantinople. In about 1037, he married Elizabeth at Novgorod.

Harald and Elizabeth went to Norway. She gave him two daughters, Maria and Ingegerd. When Harald sailed to the Orkeny Islands in 1066, he took the two girls with him, hoping to use them to win over the friendship and allegiance of some of the nobles of those islands.

In 1045, Harald married a second time. This bride was Thora, a native Norwegian. Although she was distinctly the "number two wife" after Elizabeth, Thora gave Harald two sons, Magnus and Olaf. They succeeded to the throne after his death in 1066.

whether the two planned to rendezvous when Harald reached northern England. It may be that Tostig had gone back to Flanders to drum up more support for his plans. But if they were together, there is no doubt that Harald was in command of the military force bearing down on England.

Norway lies well to the north of England. Harald sailed from Solunde, which is at about 61 degrees north latitude, and came to the English coast at Scarborough, which is close to 54 degrees north. It was an easy voyage for Norsemen accustomed to the sea, but relatively few Englishmen had ever managed the trip in the opposite direction.

When Harald arrived off the coast of northeast England, King Harold, the housecarls, and the majority of the English militia were all in Sussex and Wessex in the south, anticipating a move by Duke William of Normandy. The Viking movement had achieved complete surprise.

The first the English knew of the Vikings was on September 12, 1066 when Harald's armada descended on the port town of Scarborough. The citizens defended their town fiercely, leading Harald to sack the place in retribution. The flames that went up over Scarborough alerted Englishmen throughout the north, and probably sent the first messages to King Harold that another enemy had landed. If the news had gone south by horse, it would have taken several days to reach the king. However, it is possible that bonfires were lit and that Harold learned the bad news within one day of Harald's landing.

The Viking fleet proceeded south, then turned into the mouth of the Humber River. Sailing up the estuary and into northern England, Harald's men had an unparalleled view of the rich lands that awaited them. On about September 18, the Vikings disembarked and marched toward York, which was then the second largest city in England.

A small English force, assembled by Earl Morcar of Northumbria and Earl Edwin of Mercia, awaited the Vikings. The two armies clashed at Fulford Gate along the banks of the Derwent River. The English chronicles tell us little of the battle, so we must rely on the Norse chronicler Snorri:

> The English earls brought their army slowly down along the river in close formation. King Harald's standard was near the river, where his forces were thickest, but the thinnest and least reliable part of the line was at the dyke. The earls now advanced down the line of the dyke, and the Norwegian flank there gave way; the English went after them, thinking that the Norwegians would flee. Earl Morcar's banner was in the van.

When King Harald saw that the English flank was advancing down the dyke and was now opposite them, he sounded the attack and urged his men forward with his banner 'Land-Waster' carried in front. The Norwegian onslaught was so fierce that everything gave way before it, and a great number of the English were killed. The English army quickly broke into flight, some fleeing up the river, and others down the river; but some of them fled into the swamp, where the dead piled up so thickly that the Norwegians could cross the swamp dry-shod.

The Viking account went on to claim that Earl Morcar was slain in the battle, but this was in error. Both English earls survived the bloody battle, and one day later they met King Harald in a peace parley.

Harald was willing to be generous. Knowing that Northumbria was composed of a mixture of people of Anglo-Saxon and Danish descent, he believed he would do better to secure northern England through love than fear. Therefore, he accepted the oaths of homage tendered him by the two earls, and found that suddenly most of northern England lay in his grasp. As a condition of their prompt surrender, the earls persuaded Harald not to sack York. The Viking host camped about one mile outside the city and paused to collect itself after this victory.

The Battle of Fulford Gate had gone extremely well for the Vikings, but it is likely that they took some punishment during the course of the battle. Therefore, it made perfect sense to rest and relax, especially since there was no organized resistance left in northern England after Earl Morcar and Earl Edwin were defeated.

Harold of England was between a rock and a hard place. He learned that the Vikings had landed in the

King Harald Harada, holding the enormous axe in the center of this picture, battles with his Norsemen against the English earls at Fulford Gate. King Harald was the best-known and most-feared warrior of his day.

north, but found himself without most of his militia men; he had sent them home September 8 because there was so little food left in camp. Harold was in London when he heard the dreadful news that the Northmen had descended on Scarborough and were headed toward York.

A lesser man, or perhaps a wiser man, might have waited and let the Vikings come to him, or let Duke William attempt a landing on the southern coast. Harold was in London, center of the kingdom, and could respond to either threat as it came more clearly into view. But Harold was not the type of man to wait.

In his campaigns against the Welsh, Harold had

tested and honed to perfection a style of warfare that was uniquely his own. Disdaining the traditional emphasis on the gathering of supplies and an orderly advance, Harold believed in a rapid march and a rendezvous, followed by a shock attack on the enemy. Given the loyalty and stamina of his housecarls, Harold was able to make this system work several times; once it had culminated in the capture of the Welsh king.

Harold received the news of the Viking landing on September 20, the same day as the Battle of Fulford Gate. Hours later all of his housecarls, and as many militia as he could gather, were on their way north. It was a bold decision, followed up by one of the most impressive marches in the history of medieval warfare.

No chronicler or diarist ever described the next four days, but most likely Harold and his men traveled north on horseback to meet the Viking invaders. Whether or not they were on horseback, the speed with which they reached the north would be positively superhuman.

Late in the afternoon of September 24, 1066, Harold and the vanguard of his army reached the town of Tadcaster, about 10 miles south of York. Not only had they covered 200 miles in four days, but they had done so without alerting their Viking foes. To ensure that this secrecy continued, Harold banned anyone from leaving Tadcaster that night. No messages or tradesmen were allowed in or out of the town.

The middle and rear parts of Harold's army probably straggled in during the course of the night. When dawn came, Harold had a sizable army, perhaps 7,000 men in all. They must have been weary beyond description, but Harold gave them no rest. By nine o'clock they were on the march again.

Harold's men passed the city of York early that morning. The city had not been occupied by a Norse garrison, and the secret of Harold's arrival was safe still. Harold and his army pushed on and neared Stamford Bridge over the Derwent River around noon.

Harald Hardrada's army was in a state of mild disarray that morning. Some of the Norsemen were with Harald and Tostig on the east side of Stamford Bridge. Others were at or near the Viking ships at Ricall. Still others were strung out along the road in between the two places. Therefore, Harald and Tostig were alarmed when they saw a gathering of men approach on the west side of the Derwent River. Harald expected a small gathering of men from York to offer tribute; instead he saw the makings of an army, as described again by Snorri:

> They could see the cloud of dust raised by the horses' hooves, and below it the gleam of handsome shields and white coats of mail. King Harald halted his troops and summoned Earl Tostig, and asked him what this army could be. Earl Tostig said he thought it was likely to be a hostile force, although it was also possible that these were some of his kinsmen seeking mercy and protection from the king in exchange for their faith and fealty.

King Harold had achieved a complete surprise. Harald and Tostig did not realize the danger they were in until the English army had arrived.

Harald was in a bad spot. His men were strung out along the road between the Humber and the Derwent River. Because it was a hot day, many of them had left their armor at the camp near York, and were marching in an unruly Viking-style, out of formation, and quite likely singing and drinking.

There was no choice but to fight. An orderly withdrawal was impossible, given the rapid approach of the English. Therefore Harald decided to stake his hopes on the bridge and on a rising piece of ground on the river's eastern bank.

Snorri described the scene as the two armies reached positions where a battle might begin:

> Twenty horsemen from the English king's company of housecarls came riding up to the Norwegian lines; they were all wearing coats of mail and so were their horses. One of the riders said, "Is Earl Tostig here in this army?"
>
> Tostig replied, "There is no denying it—you can find him here." Another of the riders said, "Your brother King Harold sends you his greetings, and this message to say you can have peace and the whole of Northumbria as well. Rather than have you refuse to join him, he is prepared to give you one third of all his kingdom." The earl answered, "This is very different from all the hostility and humiliation he offered me last winter. If this offer had been made then, many a man who is now dead would still be alive, and England would now be in better state. But if I accept this offer now, what will he offer King Harald Sigurdsson for all his effort?" The rider said, "King Harold has already declared how much of England he is prepared to grant him: seven feet of ground or as much more as he is taller than other men." Earl Tostig said, "Go now and tell King Harold to make ready for battle. The Norwegians will never be able to say that Earl Tostig abandoned King Harald Sigurdsson."

The battle was soon joined.

The English had the best of it, almost from the beginning. The Viking attempt to hold the bridge failed, even though one Norwegian fighter stood like the Roman hero

Horatio at the bridge, using his great battle ax to keep the English back. One story tells that this hero was brought down by an Englishman who used a boat to come under the bridge and stab upwards. At any rate the English took the bridge and crossed to the Norwegian side of the river.

What had started as a battle had become a melee. English and Viking warriors fought each other hand-to-hand, without the benefit of the famed English shield wall. In this type of personal fighting, the Vikings were usually at their best. There were definitely some drunk men among Harald's army that day, but they had entered their drunken state in the desire for pleasure, not for battle. The fury of the traditional Viking berserker was not achieved by these revelers. In almost every way, the

This scene from the Battle of Stamford Bridge shows King Harold of England looking down at the bodies of King Harald of Norway and Earl Tostig, Harold's brother. King Harold had made good his promise that Harald Hardrada should receive only seven feet of English soil—the length of his lifeless body.

English held the upper hand in the battle.

King Harald fell sometime in the early afternoon. No record is made of how he was killed, but the warrior who had terrified foes from Russia to the Mediterranean died near Stamford Bridge, earning the seven feet of English soil he had been promised by the English heralds. Tostig too, lost his life, probably sometime after the death of Harald. By two in the afternoon, the battle had become a rout with the English winning everywhere.

All was not yet finished, however. Some of the Vikings came from their ships and made a counterattack. It was now mid-afternoon, and many of the English were weary from the struggle. The effort required to wield a battle-ax while wearing a sheet of mail is indescribable. Given that it was a warm day, the effort must have been tremendous.

The Viking counterattack was vanquished within two hours. By nightfall, the army of King Harald and Tostig lay in complete ruins—the English had won a thorough and complete victory. King Harold's gamble, his daring march north, had paid rich dividends.

The next day was spent clearing the battlefield and burying the English dead. The Viking dead were thrown into a great pile, and a chronicler reported he saw their bones as much as 100 years later. While his men engaged in this dreadful task, King Harold went to York to meet with Earls Morcar and Edwin.

History would have forgiven King Harold had he been angry and merciless toward the two earls. They had risen in rebellion against his brother one year earlier; now they had sworn allegiance to Harald of Norway after losing their battle. But the record clearly shows that Harold, like Harald before him, was inclined to be generous. He forgave the two earls and accepted their homage once more. Harold clearly needed the help and good will of the northern leaders, but this generosity was unexpected. It shows Harold to be either an extremely good-hearted man, or a brilliant strategist, or perhaps both.

Harold met also with the Viking leaders who survived the battle. Among them was Prince Olaf, the 18-year-old son of Harald. Olaf might have expected the worst, but Harold assured him of friendship for the future. A grateful Olaf led the survivors away from northern England.

The English victory had been so complete that only 24 Norse ships were needed to carry away the survivors of the Battle of Stamford Bridge.

Feasts and celebrations followed. Harold was apparently in the midst of one of these feasts when an urgent message arrived: Duke William had landed in Sussex, which was Harold's home territory. Another invasion had occurred; another enemy had to be fought.

MAR E

William Lands

Duke William's fleet sailed from Normandy on September 27, just two days after the Battle of Stamford Bridge. Duke William did not know of the events to the north; he probably experienced a good deal of anxiety during the crossing. Would King Harold and the English detect their movement?

Then came William, eorl of Normandy, into Pevensey on Michaelmas eve, and as soon as they were prepared, they built a stronghold at the town of Hastings.

—The *Anglo-Saxon Chronicle*

The late summer of 1066 was extremely vexing for Duke William of Normandy. His ships were built, his men were ready, but the wind would not oblige him. It blew steadily from the north, preventing William from sailing from the mouth of the Somme River.

Then on September 27, the wind finally shifted direction. It blew from the south. William had to take a gigantic risk. It was entirely possible that this was a temporary change in the wind; it might shift back to the north at any time. Should he embark his men, sail into the Channel, and make himself vulnerable to English scouting vessels if the wind changed?

The duke took the risk. All day on the 27th, his men hastened to the shore, bringing aboard their armor, their food and wine, and most importantly their horses. This took some work; the Bayeux Tapestry shows men cajoling horses, pulling them onto the small craft that would cross the Channel. By the late afternoon, some of the ships were still not ready, but William could not wait. He sailed aboard the *Morea*, with a lantern hung above as a signal to the rest of the fleet. By nightfall many of the Norman ships were in the Channel.

The night was full of anxiety for William and most of his captains. Navigating in the darkness was a major undertaking; it was made even more hazardous because the horses were nervous because of the choppy waves.

When dawn broke William and his crew were alone, without the rest of the fleet; there were no other ships to be seen. The navigation showed he was right on course, but that would be of little importance if he did not have support. Perhaps an hour later, his lookouts spied first three or four other ships, then a great crowd of them as the fleet caught up with its commander. The Norman chiefs breathed easier and headed for shore.

Although Hastings is the name most associated with William and the crossing, he and most of his ships came to anchor at Pevensey in East Sussex. It was a natural landing place, and it would not attract the attention that other major ports, such as Dover, might have. By late afternoon William and most of his 7,000 men were on shore. The most difficult part of the invasion had been accomplished.

The next day William was anxious for news. He did not know about King Harald's landing in the north or the

The Bayeux Tapestry shows the type of warfare that extended to the civilian population of England. A mother and son are forced to abandon their home as Norman soldiers set fire to the dwelling.

forced march that King Harold had made there. But William did know something of Tostig and the former earl's intentions; therefore, William could surmise that something might be up. There was no other way to account for his landing without any organized resistance.

One day into the landing, Duke William worked to secure the area. His men had brought the rudiments of forts, and those forts were now constructed near the coast. Other Normans were sent out to forage in the area, to bring back food and supplies.

One of the most heartrending scenes in the Bayeux Tapestry shows a woman and child leaving their home as two Normans reach up to the roof and set it ablaze. This scene sends a timeless message about the inhumanity of war and the barbarous methods by which armies terrorize civilian populations.

Even his defenders usually concede that Duke William had no need to undertake this foraging and pillage—the Normans had brought food and wine in their ships. Instead, the forage and pillage was probably a calculated effort to persuade England that it was hopeless to resist the duke and his Norman army.

Two days after landing Duke William still knew nothing about King Harold's whereabouts. Despite the remarkably close timing between their two landings (Harald Hardrada in the north and Duke William in the south), there had been no coordination between the two invaders. So, once again, Harold was able to turn his opponent's lack of knowledge into an advantage.

King Harold was at York when the news reached him that William had landed. We cannot be sure of the day, but the signal fires on the English coast may have informed him as little as two days after the event. Harold had just managed a march and battle that had finished off the most threatening Viking invasion in recent history, but he and his men had no time to rest.

Neither the *Anglo-Saxon Chronicle* nor any other English documents speak to King Harold's state of mind. All we know is that within one day of receiving the bad news, Harold and his housecarls, all on horseback, were on their way back to the city of London.

Although there was need for haste, the southern journey was probably somewhat slower than the northern one had been. Many of the housecarls had sustained wounds during the Battle of Stamford Bridge, and no one could expect them to make the remarkable speed they had achieved from south to north.

Harold and the vanguard of his army entered London on October 5, 1066. Here they recieved good news, at least. Duke William had not ventured from his beachhead; the Normans were still lodged between

Hastings and Pevensey. Harold spent the next five days gathering the Anglo-Saxon levies from the region around London. By October 10, he felt ready to proceed to Sussex and try the matter in battle.

Harold's younger brother, Earl Garyth, tried to dissuade the king. There was no need to attack the invader; let the Normans occupy Sussex all winter if they wanted. But more to the point, if there was to be a battle, let Garyth himself lead the army while Harold stayed in London. This was no time to risk the king and thereby the kingdom.

Garyth's words make excellent sense today. They may have made good sense to those who heard them at the time, except for the king. Harold had made his name and career on the success of his lightning speed and strikes. He was still elated by his victory over the Vikings in the north. Now he was ready to try again.

Much as one admires Harold for his courage, it seems clear this was a mistake. Had Harold waited even two weeks, he could have assembled an army twice as large as the one with which he left London. Because of his desire for speed and his hope that he would surprise the foe, Harold left London with less than 7,000 men, a good many of whom had fought at Stamford Bridge and were, therefore, still recuperating from the battle.

Hastings is about 70 miles south and southwest of London. Harold and his men set out the evening of October 11, with a rendezvous point named as a hoary apple tree which stood on a hill called Senlac. It is not clear whether the English army went as one body, or if it proceeded in groups and then met near the hoary apple tree. What we can say is that King Harold had in mind almost exactly the tactic that had worked against the Vikings: a rendezvous point some miles from the foe, a swift final march and surprise attack.

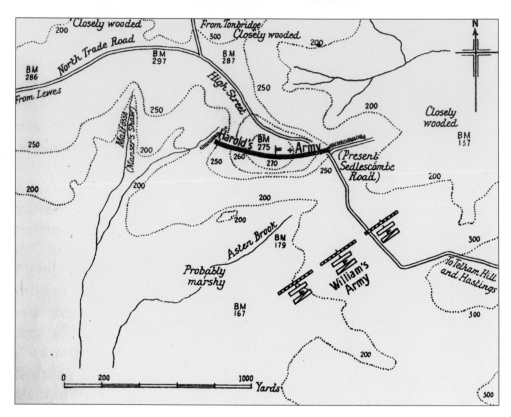

This map from J.F.C. Fuller's *Military History of the Western World,* shows that Harold and the English had chosen an excellent spot to block the Norman advance. The English are on the hill at Senlac; the Normans are advancing, but cannot maneuver around the English.

The English forces met at the rendezvous point on the evening of October 13. The king arrived and set up his personal standard, the Dragon of Wessex. King Harold conferred with his brothers (both had come with him) and perhaps had a few hours sleep that night. Harold may well have been confident. Not only had he shown himself a master of speed and surprise, but he was about to fight in Sussex, part of his earldom. This was land he knew well and which the Normans did not.

Five miles away Duke William learned of Harold's approach. It may have been late that evening or even in the early morning hours, but William was alerted. Within hours he had his entire army mobilized and on the march toward that ridge where the English had assembled. Harold had met his match in William. Neither of them would let the other take the initiative; both men wanted to be the aggressor.

Hastings

Norman cavalry, on the left, charge the English foot soldiers drawn up in their shield wall formation. One small English archer is seen on the extreme right. His diminutive size probably indicates that the English had few archers that day, October 14, 1066.

Hic William dux alloquitur suis militibus ut prepararent se viriliter et sapienter ad prelium contra Anglorum exercitum.

Here Duke William exhorts his solders that they prepare themselves manfully and wisely for the battle against the English army.

—The Bayeux Tapestry

The English and Norman armies were about equal in size—each had slightly fewer than 7,000 men. But in certain military aspects, the Normans were distinctly superior to the

English. William had many horses with him and men who were true cavalrymen accustomed to charges. The Normans also had many archers. Even though England would later make the longbow famous, Harold had few archers, and therefore the Normans could, to some extent, hit the enemy without exposing themselves.

If it was strictly a battle on foot, the English would have had the advantage. The housecarls were renowned for their skill with ax and sword, and the English militia was excellent in its use of missiles. Most importantly, the Anglo-Saxon shield wall was tested and proven as an effective device in warfare. Rather like the ancient Macedonians, who had marched in a phalanx that locked shield on shield, the Anglo-Saxons fought in close formation, using the shield wall both offensively and defensively.

Harold took one look at the Normans and knew he had made a mistake in advancing so far so fast. His foes were more mobile, and given the right moment, the Norman cavalry might shatter his shield wall and disperse his men into disparate groups. There was only one hope: to stand on the hillside and receive the enemy's attacks. Any type of offensive move would bring his men under the range of the horses' hooves.

Harold's brother urged the king once again to leave the ground, to leave command of the field to him. That way, win or lose, the English would not lose their monarch. Harold refused, as he had before. But this time Harold's intuition was probably correct. If word spread in the English lines that the king had left the field, chaos and despair might have defeated the English before William's army ever attacked.

Harold took the center position, where his personal emblem flapped in the breeze. His brothers took command of both flanks, and then the Anglo-Saxons hunkered down for the inevitable assault.

There were no flags of truce and no parleys this day. Both sides knew that blows must prevail.

William had both his personal flag and the banner which the pope had sent to bless the Norman invasion. Prior to beginning the battle, William exhorted his men. He reminded them they were on a holy mission to reclaim the Church of England, to bring it into complete conformity with that of Rome. He reminded them of the perils they had already endured in crossing the Channel, and he hinted that there was no retreat. If the Normans were to lose this battle, they would be hunted down like animals by the very people whose homes they had recently pillaged. It was all or nothing this day.

By contrast, Harold said little to his men. His followers were tried and true by this point. They had marched all the way to York and back, and had defeated the greatest Viking warrior of their era. They would not be found wanting today; the only question was whether they could endure the combination of arrows, horses, and men that the Normans would throw against them.

The battle began around nine in the morning, and historians described the scene:

> It was one of the sacred hours of the Church; it was at the hour of prime, three hours before noon-day, that the first blows were exchanged between the invaders and the defenders of England . . . Before the two armies met hand to hand, a juggler or minstrel, known as Taillefer, the Cleaver of Iron, rode forth from the Norman ranks as if to defy the whole force of England in his single person. He craved and obtained the

The Papacy

In 1066 the papacy stood at a crossroads between reform and corruption. The 200 years prior to 1066 had been difficult ones for the leaders of the Roman Catholic Church. German kings, better known as the Holy Roman Emperors, had made and unmade several pontiffs. There was a continuing tug of war between the members of the church leadership who wanted to please the Holy Roman Emperor and those who said the papacy must stand alone on its own merits.

Pope Nicholas II instituted a series of reforms, culminating in 1059. Thenceforth, pontiffs were to be elected by a college of cardinals in Rome. Abuses such as clerical pluralism, which meant holding more than one church office at a time, were punishable.

Alexander II became pope in 1061. An Italian by birth, Alexander had spent a number of years in Normandy and had been a special pupil of Lanfranc, a Norman bishop. Pope Alexander was ready to believe most of what came to him from Norman sources, and his blessing of Duke William's invasion of England seemed predestined by his affinity for Lanfranc and his compatriots.

Alexander died in 1071 and was succeeded by a monk named Hildebrand who became Pope Gregory VII. Over the next decade, Gregory VII fought a war of wits and of words with Henry IV, the Holy Roman Emperor. Henry wanted the power to name and appoint bishops; Gregory argued that this was the province only of the pontiff. The two men excoriated each other in letters and public announcements. In 1077 the emperor was forced to go to the pope's Alpine castle of Canossa and beg forgiveness for his conduct. The pope absolved Henry that day, but the struggle continued.

Gregory VII died in exile; so did Henry IV. Their long struggle resulted in a compromise under which the pope appointed bishops, but the emperor invested them with the staff and ring, symbols of their holy office.

Duke's leave to strike the first blow; he rode forth, singing songs of Roland and of Charlemagne—so soon had the name and exploits of the great German become the spoil of the enemy. He threw his sword into the air and caught it again; but he presently showed that he could use warlike weapons for other purposes than for jugglers' tricks of this kind; he pierced one Englishman with his lance, he struck down another with this sword, and then himself fell beneath the blows of their comrades. A bravado of this kind might serve as an omen, it might stir up the spirits of men on either side; but it could in no other way affect the fate of the battle.

The Norman foot soldiers made their way up the hill at Senlac. The Normans were met by a barrage of hand-held missiles, fired perhaps by slingshots, or perhaps simply hurled by the English militiamen. Some Normans fell before they reached the crest of the hill. Those who reached the level ground ran smack into the English shield wall.

This was something different for the Normans. In their many battles on the continent, they were accustomed to fighting with foes who, like themselves, were a mixture of foot, horse, and archers. They might sing ballads about meeting a shield wall, but the experience was devastating. Many Normans fell before the impact; the rest scampered down the hill. The first phase was over, a decided victory for the English.

The day was cool, a typical autumn day in England, but the armor carried by the men on both sides made for heat and exhaustion. Both sides probably rested after this first assault.

William now pressed with the second phase of the

needed to overcome the resistance of the English, diminished as were their numbers, and wearied as they were with the livelong toil of that awful day. The duke ordered his archers to shoot up in the air, that their arrows might, as it were, fall straight from heaven. The effect was immediate and fearful. No other device of the wily duke that day did such fearful execution. Helmets were pierced; eyes were put out; men strove to guard their heads with their shields, and, in so doing, they were of course less able to wield their axes

The same tactic would have failed perhaps two hours earlier, but now it was exactly on target. English men started falling out of formation, with arrows in their arms or legs. The shield wall was perilously close to disintegration.

Seeing the success of his archers, William decided to risk everything on a full frontal assault. Even the first attack of the day at nine in the morning had not carried the weight of this final assault. All the Normans, foot soldiers, cavalry, and archers made a last charge up the hill at Senlac, and this time they found much less resistance than before.

No source, not even the Bayeux Tapestry, tells us in a convincing manner what happened in this last assault. We know that the Normans mounted the hill, that there followed a hand-to-hand struggle on the ridge. But whether Harold and his brothers were killed in sword fights, or whether Harold was killed by an arrow in the eye, as many sources suggest, remains unknown.

All we can say with confidence is that in the late moments of the afternoon, just before dusk, the last English resistance collapsed. King Harold and his two brothers all died on the hill, as did more than half the men they had brought south from London. The remnants of the English

The fighting between the English under King Harold II and Duke William's Norman invaders was chaotic and violent during the Battle of Hastings. By the end of the battle, Harold would be dead and William would have a new name—William the Conqueror.

army disappeared into the coming darkness.

It was as thorough and complete a victory as William might have hoped. That, however, does not obscure how hard-fought the battle had been. Even a few lucky instances might well have tipped the battle the other way, and it would have been Duke William, his brother Odo, and their retainers who died that afternoon.

Duke William of Normandy was crowned King William I of England on December 25, 1066. The ceremony took place in Westminster Abbey. William the Bastard had long ago become Duke William of Normandy. The Duke had now become a King.

Conquest and Coronation

The voices which on the Epiphany had shouted "Yea, yea, King Harold," shouted at Christmas with equal apparent zeal "'Yea, yea, King William." Men's hearts had not changed, but they had learned, through the events of that awful year, to submit as cheerfully as might be to the doom which could not be escaped.

—History of the Norman Conquest

T he battle was over but the campaign continued. William had won his great victory and his rival was dead, but the kingdom still had to be won.

William acted cautiously in the days and weeks after the Battle of Hastings. Another man might have headed straight north, covering the 60 miles to London. But William was consistently methodical and level-headed. He would not proceed until his flanks were secure.

First, William had his men spend at least two days burying the dead. The duke also made a promise that he would build and maintain an abbey on Senlac Hill to give thanks to God for the victory. That had to wait, but the dead were buried immediately.

What happened to the remains of King Harold has long been disputed. Most chronicles agree that the corpse was violated on the evening of the battle; that Norman knights kicked and muddied the body. What happened afterward, though, remains a subject of debate. Some people assert that Harold's mother, the widow of Godwin, received her son's corpse from William. Others say the body was taken to Hastings and dumped into the sea. Because it was never proven where the body went, folk tales began to circulate that King Harold had survived the battle and continued life as a humble peasant in some village in Wessex. However, these rumors can be dismissed. Harold was dead, and the Anglo-Saxon kingdom was riven in pieces by his demise.

Within a week of the Battle of Hastings, William was on the march again. He did not make the straight overland march towards London; rather he returned to the coast and began a circuitous march that would make the port cities of southeast England his own. It was a sound strategy. By securing the port towns, William would ensure the possibility of his own retreat, if need be. But perhaps more important, he wanted to undermine the faith of the English in their leaders.

Dover surrendered without a fight, and William began to rebuild its fortifications which had fallen into decay. Dover had a lighthouse, built by the Romans 700 hundred years earlier, and William began constructing a series of new buildings around this lighthouse. Dover, standing near the narrowest part of the Channel, provided him with excellent means of communication with Normandy. It also had symbolic importance because William claimed that Harold, in his oath of 1064, agreed to support a Norman garrison there.

Canterbury also surrendered to William without a fight. Although William was a thoroughly worldly man, he knew the importance of religion and of spiritual symbols. One of the most important to the English was the church at Canterbury, which was where a delegation of Christian missionaries had first landed back in 573. Canterbury was, and remains today, deeply important to English spirituality.

By taking and occupying Canterbury, William could claim to have fulfilled his promise to Pope Alexander: that he would bring the English Church back to full conformity with the Catholic Church in Rome. Canterbury was therefore another important step in establishing legitimacy to William's reign.

Harold's death came as a swift and bitter blow to the English leaders. Archbishop Stigand, who had been one of Harold's closest advisers, was not at Canterbury when William arrived. Stigand had gone to London, where he orchestrated the selection of a new Anglo-Saxon king with Archbishop Aldred of York. The fight was not yet over and the English needed a leader.

The two archbishops did not consider Harold's sons as possible successors. The old stigma of Harold's family, and his lack of connection to the throne through blood, now resurfaced in the wake of his defeat. Rather than Harold's kin, the two archbishops looked back to the time of King Edward the Confessor, and even further back to his grandfather Ethelred the Unready. The only remaining member of that family, the Cedric line, was Edgar the Atheling.

Major Leaders of the 10th and 11th Centuries

Aldred:	Archbishop of York, 1060-1069; crowned both Harold and William
Alexander II:	Pope, 1062-1073
Baldwin of Flanders:	Count of Flanders, mid-11th century
Canute:	King of Denmark and England, 1016-1035
Charles III ("the Simple"):	King of France, 898-929
Edgar the Aetheling:	Grandson of Edmund Ironside, briefly King of England, October-December 1066
Edith:	Daughter of Godwin; married King Edward the Confessor
Edmund Ironside:	Prince of England who fought Canute, 1014-1016
Edward the Confessor:	King of England, 1042-1066
Elizabeth:	Daughter of duke of Novgorod, Russia; married Harald Hardrada of Norway
Emma:	Daughter of duke of Normandy; married King Ethelred of England in 1002
Godwin:	Earl of Wessex, 1040-1053
Gregory VII:	Pope, 1073-1085
Count Guy:	Count of Ponethieu; captured Harold Godwinson
Harald Hardrada:	Viking adventure; king of Norway, 1045-1066
Harold Godwinson:	Son of Godwin; earl of Wessex; king of England, 1066
Tostig Godwinson:	Son of Godwin; earl of Northumbria, 1055-1065
Gryth Godwinson:	Son of Godwin; earl of East Anglia
Leofric Godwinson:	Son of Godwin; earl of Mercia
Lanfranc:	Bishop of Bec, Normandy; tutor to Pope Alexander II
Malcolm Canmore:	King of Scotland, 1057-1093
Morcar:	Earl of Northumbria, 1065-1066
Odo:	Half-brother of Duke William; bishop of Bayeux
Olaf II:	King of Norway, 1015-1030; became St. Olaf in 1041
Olaf III:	King of Norway, 1069-1093; called Olaf the Peaceful
Richard the Fearless:	Duke of Normandy; father of Emma of Normandy
Richard II of Normandy:	Duke of Normandy; brother of Emma
Robert of Normandy:	Duke of Normandy; father of William of Normandy; died while returning from pilgrimage to Jerusalem in 1035
Rollo:	Viking adventurer; first duke of Normandy, around 911
Stigand:	Archbishop of Canterbury, 1052-1072
William of Normandy:	Duke of Normandy, 1035-1087; king of England, 1066-1087

Edgar was the grandson of Edmund Ironsides and only just beyond boyhood. He had yet to serve in—much less lead—a military campaign. All common sense argued against placing an untried boy on the throne, but common sense was overridden by the need to show a legitimate descent from the English royal family. Edgar became king in name sometime in November, although he never had a coronation ceremony.

It is unknown whether the new king could have become a ruler given the time. He had no time because Duke William was closing the net around London.

William left Canterbury sometime in November. Again, as after Hastings, he did not take the most direct route. Rather than approach London, William marched his army west, keeping well to the south of the Thames River. Only when he was a good 40 miles west of London did William and the Normans cross, probably at Wallingford. Once on the north side of the river, William began a slow, methodical approach on London.

Clearly, Duke William did not relish the thought of a siege. London was too large; its population too militant. Even should he win such a siege, William did not want to make martyrs of those who resisted him. So he inched closer day by day and was gratified to see the resistance melt before him. Even Archbishop Stigand came to kiss William's hand on his march, and by the time he reached the capital city, there was no need to fight.

This relatively bloodless taking of London shows the best qualities in Duke William's arsenal: his patience and forethought. The city was his; now he would claim the throne and realm.

Edgar the Atheling was abandoned by the same men who had proclaimed him king just six weeks before. William met with the leaders of London, and they agreed upon a coronation ceremony set for Christmas Day, 1066.

The White Tower, built by Norman craftsmen after the Conquest, is the central part of today's Tower of London complex. The Normans brought white stone from Caen, Normandy, rather than work with English materials.

William chose to receive the crown in Westminster Abbey, rather than in the heart of the old city. His reason was sound; he wanted more than ever to appear the legitimate heir to Edward the Confessor, and he could do so by being crowned in the church Edward had built. Though there was no sound of alarm prior to the ceremony, there

were Norman soldiers throughout the church and sur-
rounding the area:

> The Christmas morn at last came; and once more,
> as on the day of the Epiphany, a king-elect entered
> the portals of the West Minster to receive his
> Crown. But now, unlike the day of the Epiphany,
> the approach to the church was kept by a guard
> of Norman horsemen. Otherwise all was peaceful
> . . . The voices which on the Epiphany had shouted
> "Yea, yea, King Harold," shouted at Christmas
> with equal apparent zeal "Yea, yea, King William."
> Men's hearts had not changed, but they had
> learned, through the events of that awful year, to
> submit as cheerfully as might be to the doom which
> could not be escaped

It was settled, as far as London was concerned. *Duke*
William, who had been called William the *Bastard* in his
youth, was now *King* William, first of his name.

Soon after the coronation, King William began building
a new Norman castle on the north bank of the Thames
River, in the old part of London. Stone was quarried at
Caen and shipped across the Channel to form what became
known as the White Tower. Today it is still the central part
of the complex known as the Tower of London.

Northern parts of England did not immediately agree
to the new king's reign. While they had no one of the old
royal line to adhere to, many people in Mercia and
Northumbria held out for two or three years before
submitting to King William. As a consequence, William
conducted campaigns in the north that ravaged the
countryside and firmly established himself as the most
ruthless leader of the age.

King William's reign brought lasting changes to England, including a stricter feudal system and centralized rule. William also became the wealthiest king in Western Europe by instituting a thorough accounting and taxation of English property.

Lasting Effects:
Changes in Government, Architecture, Language, and Culture

Second only to the crowning of Charles the Great, William's victory at Hastings, which led to his own crowning—also on Christmas Day— was the greatest event of the Middle Ages.

—A Military History of the Western World, Volume One

How did such a small battle, fought between a total of 14,000 men, have such an effect on Western Europe? That question has been debated time and again, and most historians have agreed that the events of October 14, 1066, had a profound and far-reaching effect on Western history.

First came changes in government. King William introduced a tighter, stricter form of feudalism to England. During the 20 years prior to the conquest, William had become a master of using the centralized feudal system in Normandy. What he brought to England was the concept of one overlord and many lesser lords, without any interconnections between them. Thus, each and every nobleman in England swore fealty directly to King William; none were allowed to swear to a count or duke, who then passed on their allegiance to the king.

Prior to the conquest, Anglo-Saxon England had been loosely governed. There had been a powerful affection on the part of the people for the throne, but the council of the nobles, the Anglo-Saxon witan, had reserved many rights to itself. Powerful earls like Harold Godwinsson had been able to govern their own estates in a semi-autonomous manner. All that changed with the appearance of the Normans and the coronation of William.

William was the first king of England to apply the principle that all the land in the realm belonged first to the monarch. He could allot sections of it and receive the traditional fealty from great lords for doing so, but everything belonged to the king and was for his use. Some of William's descendants applied this quite literally, and made it difficult for many of their subjects to hunt and fish in the manner to which they were accustomed. The activities of the legendary Robin Hood and his band in Sherwood Forest were in response to the tight restrictions imposed by William and the Normans.

There were changes in architecture as well. As he consolidated his hold on England, King William showed a distinct preference for castles and for those castles to be built in white Norman stone.

William's Norman past had serious consequences for England and France. William retained his position as duke of Normandy when he became king of England. Therefore, William was technically a vassal of the king of France, while he was also leader of England. This clear conflict in loyalties meant that most of William's successors lived what might almost be called double lives, culturally speaking. They lived part of the time in England, and part of the time in Normandy, and many of them remained quite French in their outlook. Even one of the greatest of all English heroes, Richard the Lion Heart (Richard la Coeur de Ligne) spoke French as his first language and English as his second.

Language changed as well. Until the Norman conquest, England was a land which mixed Teutonic and Scandinavian tongues. The result was the Anglo-Saxon spoken prior to 1066, and it remained the basis for the English language. But many new words, French words, entered the language, and the result can be seen even today.

There were also changes in information and the exchange of knowledge. King William knew the importance of taxation; therefore he wanted to know the holdings of all his new subjects. He conceived, and his officials directed, the compilation of the *Domesday Book*, which calculated and assessed all of English property in the year 1086, as described in the *Anglo-Saxon Chronicle*:

> He then sent his men over all England into each shire, and had it made out how many hides of land were in the shire; what the king himself had in land, and in livestock on the land; what dues he had from property each twelve months from the shire; also he let it be written down how much land his archbishops had, his diocesan bishops, his abbots and his eorls—though I tell it lewngthily—what and how much each man who was holding land in England, in land, in livestock, and how much money it was worth. So very closely did he let it be searched out that there was not a single hide nor

rod of land—nor, further, it shameful to tell, though it
seemed to him no shame to do it—not an ox, a cow, a
pig was left out, that was not set in his document; and
all the documents were brought to him afterwards

By this means, King William became the most powerful
and the wealthiest king in Western Europe, not so much
because England was rich, but because the king knew his
subject's property worth and could therefore tax them to
the fullest extent possible.

One of the best examples of the information in the
Domesday Book concerns land that had once belonged to
Earl Godwin, father of King Harold:

"Gilbert son of Richer de Aigle holds Witley. Earl
Godwin held it. Then it was assessed for 20 hides, now for
12 hides. There is land for 16 ploughs. In demesne are 2
ploughs; and there are 37 villeins and 3 cottars with 13
ploughs. A church there and 3 acres of meadow. Wood for
30 pigs. In the time of King Edward and afterwards, it was
worth 15 pounds; now 16 pounds" (*Domesday Re-Bound*).

The *Domesday Book* portrays a people, a land, and a
society. The book gives us the single best look at economic
life in the Middle Ages.

Norway also experienced changes. It was a shattered
Viking fleet that limped away from the Battle of Stamford
Bridge. Some records say it took only 24 of the 240 vessels to
carry the survivors to Norway. Among them was Prince
Olaf, the younger son of Harald Hardrada.

For the next two years Magnus and Olaf, the two sons
of Harald, were co-rulers of Norway. There was no way to
appreciate the differences caused by the Battle of Stamford
Bridge until 1069, when Magnus died, leaving Olaf the sole
king of Norway.

It is impossible to say whether it was the failed invasion that influenced him, but we know that King Olaf III

turned out to be as different a ruler from his father as could possibly be imagined. Governing Norway from 1069 until his death in 1093, King Olaf never fought a battle, much less a war. He became known as "Olaf the Pacific" or Olaf the Peaceful.

These were prosperous and contented times in Norway. King Olaf altered some of the living conditions at the palace in Trondheim. For the first time in Norwegian history, rooms of the palace had their separate stoves for heat, and Norwegian nobles drank from beakers rather than horns. All together, it may be said that Olaf represented a dramatic break with the past, and that Norway came to be seen less as a Viking power and more as the furthest north bastion of Christian Europe.

The original Domesday Book is held at the Public Record office in London. Information about houses, land, cattle, and people allowed William the Conqueror and his successors to define and tax the holdings of their subjects.

The Bayeux Tapestry was woven sometime in the 20 years after the Battle of Hastings. Seeing the remarkable portrait it made of such an important event, we can give it the honor it deserves. Still today, the tapestry unfolds before the viewer much as a song or an opera unfolds to its listeners.

1000	Danish attacks on England and Normandy increase
1002	King Ethelred of England marries Emma, daughter of the duke of Normandy
1015	Harald Sigurdsson, younger half-brother of King Olaf, born in Norway
1016	King Etheldred dies as Danish attacks increase; Danish leader Canute wins Battle of Ashingdon in October; Canute the Great becomes king of England
1017	Canute marries Emma of Normandy, the widow of King Ethelred
1023	Harold Godwinson born in Wessex, southeast England
1027	William the Bastard born in Falaise, Normandy
1030	King Olaf of Norway dies in Battle of Stilkestad; Harald Sigurdsson left Norway to become a Viking adventurer in Russia and Constantinople

1064
Earl Harold goes to
Normandy and swears
an oath of allegiance to
Duke William.

1065
Tostig deposed as
earl of Northumbria

1064

1065

Timeline

1035	Canute dies; succeeded by son Harthacanute
1035	Duke Robert of Normandy dies; succeeded by son William
1041	The deceased King Olaf becomes a saint. He remains the patron saint of Norway to this day.
1042	Edward the Confessor becomes King of England
1047	Duke William wins the Battle of Val-el-Dunes and becomes duke in the fullest sense of the title
1051	King Edward the Confessor exiles Earl Godwin and his family
1052	Earl Godwin and his family returns to England and the king's good grace
1053	Godwin, progenitor of the Godwin family, dies in King Edward's presence
1055	Tostig Godwinsson becomes Earl of Northumbria

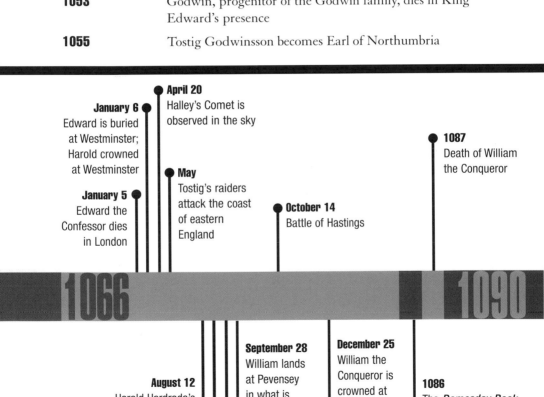

April 20
Halley's Comet is observed in the sky

January 6
Edward is buried at Westminster; Harold crowned at Westminster

January 5
Edward the Confessor dies in London

May
Tostig's raiders attack the coast of eastern England

October 14
Battle of Hastings

1087
Death of William the Conqueror

1066

1090

August 12
Harald Hardrada's fleet leaves Norway

September 28
William lands at Pevensey in what is now Sussex

December 25
William the Conqueror is crowned at Westminster

1086
The *Domesday Book* is complied. It shows land, people, houses, and animals throughout England

September 20
Battle of Fulford Gate

September 25
Battle of Stamford Bridge

1059	College of cardinals is created in Rome
1064	Earl Harold goes to Normandy and swears an oath of allegiance to Duke William
1065	Tostig deposed as earl of Northumbria
1066	
January 5	Edward the Confessor dies in London
January 6	Edward is buried at Westminster; Harold crowned at Westminster
April 20	Halley's Comet is observed in the sky
May	Tostig's raiders attack the coast of eastern England
August 12	Harald Hardrada's fleet leaves Norway
September 20	Battle of Fulford Gate
September 25	Battle of Stamford Bridge
September 28	William lands at Pevensey in what is now Sussex
October 14	Battle of Hastings
December 25	William the Conqueror is crowned at Westminster
1067	Prince Olaf and Prince Magnus become co-rulers of Norway
1069	Upon Prince Magnus' death, Olaf becomes King Olaf III
1086	The *Domesday Book* is compiled. It shows land, people, houses, and animals throughout England.
1087	Death of William the Conqueror

Brown, R. Allen. *The Normans and the Norman Conquest.* The Boydell Press, 1968.

Freeman, Edward A., M.A., Hon. D.C.L. *The History of the Norman Conquest of England, Its Causes and its Results.* Oxford: The Clarendon Press, 1873.

Fuller, J.F.C., Major General. *A Military History of the Western World.* Minerva Press, 1954.

Her Majesty's Stationery Office. *Domesday Re-Bound.* London, 1954.

Higham, N.J. *The Death of Anglo-Saxon England.* Sutton Publishing, 1997.

Lloyd, Alan. *The Making of the King: 1066.* Holt, Rinehart and Winston, 1966.

Magnus Magnusson and Hermann Palsson, translators and editors. *King Harald's Saga*, from Snorri Sturlson's *Heimskringla.* Penguin Books, 1966.

Patterson, Benton Rain. *Harold and William: The Battle for England, A.D. 1064-1066.* Cooper Square Press, 2001.

Savage, Anne, translator and collator. *The Anglo-Saxon Chronicles.* St. Martin's Press, 1983.

Stenton, Sir Frank et al., general editors. *The Bayeux Tapestry: A Comprehensive Survey.* Phaidon Publishers Inc., 1957.

Wood, Michael. *In Search of the Dark Ages.* Facts on File Publications, 1987.

page:

2: Reprinted from "The Anglo-Saxon Chronicle" Pheobe Phillips/William Heinemann
6: Scala/Art Resource, NY
11: Werner Forman/Art Resource, NY
12: Hulton Archive by Getty Images
14: Hulton Archive by Getty Images
19: Reprinted from "The Anglo-Saxon Chronicle" Phoebe Phillips/William Heinemann
21: Hulton Archive by Getty Images
24: Werner Forman/Art Resource, NY
28: Werner Forman/Art Resource, NY
32: Werner Forman/Art Resource, NY
34: Reprint from "The Anglo Saxon Chronicle" N.J. Higham
39: Werner Forman/Art Resource, NY
40: Werner Forman/Art Resource, NY

42: Werner Forman/Art Resource, NY
45: Hulton Archive by Getty Images
51: Werner Forman/Art Resource, NY
54: Hulton Archive by Getty Images
60: Reprint from "The Anglo-Saxon Chronicle" N.J. Higham
65: Hulton Archive by Getty Images
68: Werner Forman/Art Resource, NY
71: Werner Forman/Art Resource, NY
74: Reprint from "Military History of the Western World," J.F.C. Fuller
76: Erich Lessing/Art Resource, NY
83: Erich Lessing/Art Resource, NY
87: Hulton Archive of Getty Images
88: Hulton Archive by Getty Images
94: Jonathon Blair/Corbis
96: Hulton Archive by Getty Images
101: Michael Furman/Corbis

Cover: © Nik Wheeler/Corbis

SAMUEL WILLARD CROMPTON is a historian with special interests in military and cultural history. He is the author or editor of more than 15 books, with subjects that range from wars that shaped world history to lighthouses and spiritual leaders of the world. Mr. Crompton teaches both American history and Western civilization at Holyoke Community College in Massachusetts.